Trip

by

Phyllis Nagy

UK première
Southwark Playhouse
September 2002

SOUTHWARK PLAYHOUSE

LONDON ARTS

Trip's Cinch was commissioned and produced by the Actors Theatre of Louisville at the 18th Annual Humana Festival of New American Plays in 1994.

Southwark Playhouse

Southwark Playhouse will be 10 years old in 2003. Since 1993 we have helped shape the regeneration of Bankside. Situated in a warehouse at the end of one of the few remaining Victorian courtyards in SE1, our atmospheric and intimate space allows us to present traditional plays such as *Othello, The Old Curiosity Shop*, and *The Winter's Tale* as well as an exciting mix of new writing, modern classics and music drama.

We are committed to encouraging an emerging generation of directors, writers and designers. We have supported companies such as The Lab (*The Woman Who Swallowed a Pin*), Tiata Fahodzi (*Abyssinia*), Wonderful Beast (*Maps of Desire*). Plays by Nell Leyshon, Stephen Sharkey and David Spencer have had their London premieres at Southwark Playhouse. We have given young directors the opportunity to explore modern classics by Peter Gill, C.P. Taylor, Jean Anouilh and Edward Bond. Our two previous artistic directors, Mehmet Ergen and Erica Whyman, have gone on to head The Arcola and The Gate Theatre.

Under our current artistic director, Thea Sharrock, we have consolidated our position as one of London's most impressive small theatres. With increased public funding we are now able to support more companies and directors, commission new work and take our productions beyond Southwark.

Education and community work is an integral part of our artistic vision. Nearly all productions have an accompanying education programme. Talented directors and actors take their skills into the classrooms of Lambeth and Southwark significantly raising achievement, enhancing awareness of language and awakening children to the joy of theatre.

Cast

BENJAMIN TRIP	**Marcus D'Amico**
VAL GRECO	**Bernice Stegers**
LUCY PARKS	**Ruth Gemmell**

Creative and Production Team

Director	**Thea Sharrock**
Designer	**Rachel Blues**
Lighting Designer	**David Plater**
Assistant Director	**Jennie Fellows**
Production Manager	**Bendy Ashfield**
Stage Manager	**Nicole Keighly**
Voice Coach	**Neil Swain**
Production Photography	**Pau Ros**
Press Representative	**Ewan Thomson and Charlotte Franklin**

Cast Biographies

Marcus D'Amico BENJAMIN TRIP

Olivier Award nominated for his work in *Angels in America* in the West End, Marcus's recent theatre work includes a tour of *Amy's View*, before which he played Cassius in David Lan's production of *Julius Caesar* for the Young Vic. Marcus's other theatre work includes *Cain* for the RSC, and the West End productions of *Design For Living* and *An Inspector Calls*. He has just played Philip Chandler in *The Bill* and other recent television work includes *Undercover Cops* for Channel 4. His film work includes Stanley Kubrick's *Full Metal Jacket*.

Bernice Stegers VAL GRECO

Theatre includes *The Idiot* (Riverside), *Murder* and *Venetia* (Gate Theatre), *A Woman of No Importance* (Cambridge Theatre Company). Television includes *Tipping the Velvet* (Sally Head Productions), *The Rag Nymph* (Festival Films), *Family Money* (Whistling Gypsy Productions), *Little Lord Fauntleroy, A Dark Adapted Eye, To Play the King* (BBC), *Kissing the Gunner's Daughter – Ruth Rendell* (Blue Heaven). Film includes *Four Weddings and a Funeral* (Working Title), *Quartet* (Merchant Ivory) and *City of Women.*

Ruth Gemmell LUCY PARKS

Film includes *Fever Pitch.* Shorts*: Perfect, Everywhere, A Stiff Drink*. Television: *Inspector Lynley Mysteries, Waking the Dead, Dalziel and Pascoe, Miller Shorts, SilentWitness* (BBC), *Blue Dove, Four Fathers, Band of Gold.* Theatre includes: *Kick for Touch* (Sheffield Crucible)*, Ancient Lights, Nabokov's Gloves* (Hampstead *Theatre*), *The Weir* (Royal Court)*, Turn of the Screw, Othello, Measure for Measure, Uncle Vanya, An Ideal Husband, The Winter's Tale, The Second Mrs Tanqueray, The Importance of Being Earnest, Tis Pity She's a Whore, The Country Wife, A Tale of Two Cities* (Queen's Theatre, Hornchurch). Ruth has also done extensive radio work.

Creative Team Biographies

Phyllis Nagy *Playwright*

Phyllis Nagy's plays include *Never Land, The Strip, Disappeared, Weldon Rising* (Royal Court Theatre); *Butterfly Kiss* (Almeida Theatre); and adaptations of Nathaniel Hawthorne's *The Scarlet Letter* (Classic Stage Company, New York) and Patricia Highsmith's *The Talented Mr Ripley* (Palace Theatre Watford). Her work for radio includes *Delores*, a contemporary version of Euripides's *Andromache* (The Sunday Play, BBC Radio 3). She is currently under commission to the Royal National Theatre, the Royal Court Theatre and the Royal Shakespeare Company.

Thea Sharrock *Director*

Thea Sharrock is the Artistic Director of Southwark Playhouse. She trained at the Anna Scher Theatre and the Market Theatre Johannesburg. Previous credits include *Free* by Simon Bowen (Loft, NT), *Top Girls* by Caryl Churchill (BAC, UK tours, Aldwych West End), *The Sleepers Den* by Peter Gill (Southwark Playhouse) and as Associate Director, *Art* by Yasmina Reza (West End & UK tour). Thea was the recipient of the James Menzies-Kitchin Memorial Trust's Young Director of the Year Award 2000 for which she first directed *Top Girls* at the BAC.

Rachel Blues *Designer*

Rachel trained at Edinburgh College of Art and Bristol Old Vic Theatre School. Recent designs include *Free* and *Life After Life* (Loft, NT), *Krindlekrax* (Birmingham Rep/Nottingham Playhouse), *Silence, Belonging* and *Winnie the Witch* (Birmingham Rep), *Loveplay* (RSC), *Top Girls* (Oxford Stage Company, UK tours and West End), *Ham* (New Vic, Stoke) *The Dove* (Warehouse, Croydon), *Bouncers* (Octagon Theatre, Bolton), *Car* (Theatre Absolute), *Intimate Death* (Gate, London), *Private Lives* and *Charley's Aunt* (Swan, Worcester). Rachel was resident designer at the Coliseum Theatre, Oldham for two years where she designed nine productions.

David Plater *Lighting Designer*

David trained at RADA. His work at the Donmar Warehouse includes *Frame 312, Three Days of Rain, Morphic Resonance, Splash Hatch, Summer Begins, Badfinger, The Other Side of the Rainbow.* He has also designed *Amy's View* (Windsor/Guildford/Tour), *What You Get & What You Expect* (Lyric Hammersmith), *What Now Little Man* (Greenwich Theatre), *Dark Tales* (Arts Theatre), *The Dave Strassman Show* (Apollo West End), *Love on the Dole* (Oldham Coliseum, Theatre Royal Hanley & Tour), *The Relationship, Island Sea, Falling Through* (Riverside Studios Hammersmith), *Girls were made to Love & Kiss* (Old Fire Station Oxford), *Oliver!* (Kircaldy & Edinburgh, N.Y.M.T.), *Count Ory* (New Sussex Opera Brighton, Eastbourne & Broomhill), *One Last Surviving, Entertaining Strangers* & *Dark of the Moo*) (Lyric Studio Hammersmith), *Cherry Orchard* (Capitol Theatre Horsham), *The Nun, Out in the Cold, The Green Parakeet, Erasmus Montanus, A Spanner in the Works, The Will, And Women Must Weep, Spring Awakening* (Greenwich Studio Theatre Company), *Metamorphosis, A Thought in 3 Parts* (BAC), *The Niss* (Edinburgh), and *Eskimo Sisters* (Southwark Playhouse). David also designs for RADA and The Royal Academy of Dance.

Jennie Fellows *Assistant Director*

Jennie trained at the University of East Anglia and East 15 Acting School. Assisting includes *Oneminutesilence* for ATC (Young Vic) and *Penthisilea* by Tom Kempinski (New End). Directing includes *The Wake* (Soho Theatre Studio) and *Tight Rope Walking* (Cockpit Theatre) both by Lucy Moore.

Nicole Keighley *Stage Manager*

Nicole studied English and Theatre Arts at Goldsmiths College. Stage Management credits include *The People Are Friendly* and *International Residency 2002* (Royal Court), *Eskimo Sisters, Maps of Desire, Macbeth* and *Charlie Lavender* (Southwark Playhouse), *The Wild Duck* and *Cloudburst* (Pentameters) and a charity production of *Midsummer Night's Dream* in Soho.

Southwark Playhouse

We are grateful to all our volunteers for their continuing support

Southwark Playhouse
62 Southwark Bridge Road
London SE1 0AS

Box Office 0207 620 3494
Admin 0207 652 2224 *Fax* 0207 261 1271

Email admin@southwarkplayhouse.co.uk
Website www.southwarkplayhouse.co.uk

Southwark Playhouse Theatre Company Limited
Registered in England 2994954
Registered Charity No 1042870

Phyllis Nagy
Trip's Cinch

ff

faber and faber

First published in the United States in 1994
by the Dramatic Publishing Company
311 Washington Street, Woodstock
IL 60098, USA

First published in the UK in 2002
by Faber and Faber Limited
3 Queen Square, London WC1N 3AU

Typeset by Country Setting, Kingsdown, Kent CT14 8ES
Printed in England by Intype London Ltd

A CIP record for this book
is available from the British Library

ISBN 0-571-21806-7

2 4 6 8 10 9 7 5 3 1

Trip's Cinch was commissioned and produced by the Actors Theatre of Louisville at the 18th Annual Humana Festival of New American Plays in March 1994.
The cast was as follows:

Benjamin Trip Steven Culp
Val Greco Barbara eda-Young
Lucy Parks Mary Schultz

Director Lisa Peterson
Scenic Designer Paul Owen
Costume Designer Esther Marquis
Lighting Designer Mary Louise Geiger
Sound Designer Casey L. Warren

Characters

Benjamin Trip
Mid-thirties.
He is quite handsome, utterly charming and groomed in a manner that suggests great old wealth.

Lucy Parks
Early- to mid-thirties.
Strong, good-looking and very sure of herself. Her barbed wit is dry and measured rather than overtly hostile.

Val Greco
Mid- to late-forties.
Opinionated, charismatic, formidable academic.

Time
The present.

Place
Somewhere along the East Coast of America.

Note
At no time should the dialogue overlap. Though the characters frequently cut each other off, no two characters ever speak simultaneously.

The Setting

A non-naturalistic landscape which is covered almost entirely by sand. It is as if there has been a blizzard of sand: high sand banks, drifts, etc. Beyond the sand, there is a clear, black night sky, stretching as far as the eye can see.

In Scene One an executive desk and two office chairs should be placed in this landscape as if they've always been there.

In Scene Two the desk and chairs are replaced with a simple kitchen table and two straight-back chairs which are placed in exactly the same position as the desk and chairs in Scene One.

In Scene Three the table and chairs are replaced by the kind of small, round bar table and chairs that are found at outdoor clubs.

Scene One

Val is bent over the desk. Trip stands behind her.

Trip Stand on your left leg.

Val lifts her right leg, bending it at the knee.

Val Like this?

Trip Hold it straight out. Like this.

He extends Val's leg out as straight as it will go. He holds on to her leg. Pause.

Val What are you doing now?

Trip I'm checking for runs in your stocking.

Val Do you find any?

Trip No. But I check for a long time. Like this.

Trip runs his hand up and down Val's leg. He takes his time.

You may relax your leg now.

Val does.

Val Thank you.

Trip You have lovely legs.

Val I don't. But thanks anyway.

A beat.

Is that right?

Trip Yes. Ask me to come closer.

Val Now?

Trip Yes.

Val Without further *prelude*?

Trip Yes.

Val Just: come closer?

Trip Yes. Please say it.

Val Come closer.

Trip I'm there.

Trip is pressed against Val.

Val Can anyone see us? Are we being watched?

Trip It's past closing time.

Val The staff?

Trip They're discreet.

Val So we can't be seen.

Trip Ask me again: come closer.

Val You can't come *much* closer. You can't *move*.

Trip I can move. Ask me.

Val Move.

A beat.

Please.

A pause.

What are you doing now?

Trip I'm listening to you cry.

Val I'm crying? I'm *upset*?

Trip You're relieved. Happy. Grateful. Tell me you're grateful.

Val Are you sure? I mean, are you really sure about this?

Trip Yes.

Val All right, then.

A beat.

I'm grateful.

Trip You have lovely legs.

Val I'm so . . . so . . . fucking *grateful.*

Trip No.

Val I'm *not* grateful?

Trip You don't swear.

Val Ah. Of course. I'm sorry.

Trip I'm slipping my hand beneath your skirt.

Val Do I resist?

Trip You cry.

Val More gratefulness.

Trip You're wet.

Val I'm *hot*?

Trip I'm *touching* you. I generate great heat.

Val So. I'm crying. I'm wet. I'm hot. What else?

Trip Tell me how hard I am.

Val How hard *are* you?

Trip I'm the hardest you've felt. Tell me.

Val (*flatly*) Okay. You're the hardest.

Trip You have lovely legs.

Val Is that *all*?

Trip Pardon?

Val You tell me I have lovely legs three times. Am I unlovely everywhere else?

Trip (*after a beat*) It's the heat of the moment. I say whatever comes to mind.

Val Oh.

Trip I'm overcome.

Val And am I still crying?

Trip Yes. It excites me.

Val You're already the hardest I've ever felt. You can't get more excited than that.

Trip Don't talk. Cry.

Val Okay.

A pause.

What next?

Trip I wait.

Val For what?

Trip You ask me to make love to you.

Val *I* ask *you*?

Trip You have to invite me inside.

Val Like a vampire. Right.

Trip Ask me.

Val What do I say? *Enter* me? Is that what I say?

Trip Yes.

Val Fine.

A beat.

Enter me.

Trip I'm there.

A pause. Trip backs away from Val.

I'm done.

Val rises and turns to Trip. She begins to laugh.

You don't laugh.

Val (*can't help herself*) No, no, I – of *course course* I don't laugh – of *course*. I mean, well, I find this all a bit difficult to –

Trip You don't *laugh*.

Val Yes yes, but it's difficult to believe, if not *impossible* to to –

Trip Nonetheless.

A beat.

There is no laughter.

Val (*stops laughing*) I'm terribly sorry.

A pause. Trip removes a handkerchief from his breast pocket and begins methodically to wipe his hands clean.

Is there something . . . wrong . . . is there, I don't know, did you dirty yourself?

Trip Yes.

Val Then? That night? You you . . . *came* . . . in your hands?

Trip No.

Val What? What then?

A pause. Trip folds his handkerchief neatly and replaces it in his breast pocket.

Trip Miss Parks did not laugh when we made love.

Val So the trial transcripts –

Trip The trial is completed. I am telling you –

Val Yes yes, but the trial is a matter of –

Trip You mustn't rely on transcripts. Human error contributes –

Val – a matter of public *record.*

A pause.

The trial transcript is a matter of public record, Mr Trip. It is an invaluable research tool.

Trip It might be wrong. The transcriber might have made errors. Don't believe everything you read.

Val Are you telling me that the transcript is incorrect? That that it's, I don't – is it *flawed*?

Trip There could be mistakes.

Val So you're saying the transcriber possibly, what? Fucked up? She fucked up the transcript?

Trip (*after a beat*) Greco. That's an Italian name.

Val Yes. Sicilian.

Trip Sicily. Cows. Volcanoes. Poverty.

Val (*after a beat*) *I* wasn't born there.

Trip What is the saying? You can take a girl out of Sicily . . .

A pause.

Val She was bent over a . . . what was it? A small sand dune?

Trip Your train of thought is very scattered, Ms Greco. It *is* Ms Greco, no?

Val Lucy Parks. That night. A couple of G and Ts in the Club Fortune. You walked along the beach. Listened to the waves. It was clear. The sky was full of stars. She bent over a small sand dune to show you the runs in her stocking.

A beat.

I am unmarried. Yes.

A pause.

Trip Do you research all your books in this manner?

Val I research. I inquire.

Trip But I don't suppose you've researched them in quite this way.

Val No. No, it's not – ordinarily, I'm speaking of my usual methods here – *ordinarily*, I write about the dead.

Trip Byron. Shelley. Elvis Presley.

Val Among others. I've done others.

Trip So *ordinarily* your subjects are unavailable to you. To speak to, that is.

Val I couldn't re-enact Shelley's drowning with him. If that's what you mean.

A pause. Trip takes a brand new deck of cards, still in its box and cellophane wrapper, from his inside jacket pocket and places it on the table.

Trip Where was it you said you teach? Bakersfield? Cleveland?

Val Minneapolis.

Trip How delightful, I'm sure.

Val The home of Prince. There's plenty of booze and bingo halls. What more could I ask?

Trip The Ivy League.

Val Been there. Seen that, Mr Trip.

A beat.

What's with the cards?

Trip My secretary has read me your essays on popular culture.

Val I hadn't thought of them as bedtime stories.

Trip They're appalling.

Val Does your secretary tuck you in as well as read to you?

Trip Though I must admit your theories on – and I can't recall your precise phrase – the supremacy of the male libido and the necessity for its its –

Val Unfettered appetite.

Trip Thank you – its unfettered appetite – is crucial to the optimal development of western civilisation.

A beat. Trip unwraps the cellophane wrapper from the deck of cards, puts the box back on the table and puts the wrapper in his jacket pocket.

Or perhaps it was all civilisation.

A pause.

Val No no. Western civilisation. That's right.

Trip Interesting. If a bit laughable.

Val I beg your pardon but –

Trip I am merely expressing my opinion. You understand I have the greatest respect for your intellect and of course I can't can't really say what –

Val – but if you would articulate your position more clearly, Mr Trip. If you could –

Trip I am incapable of *articulating*. I leave that to those of you who write books. I act on impulse.

Trip removes the cards from their box and begins to shuffle them slowly and deliberately.

Val Fair enough.

Trip I see a beautiful car: I buy it. I see a beggar in the street and I cross to avoid him.

Val No no, fair enough. All right.

Trip Most people, Ms Greco, the *majority* of people are not even self-aware enough to realise that they act on impulse. They actually believe they think out their decisions rationally and with great care. This, they believe, is civilised behaviour.

A beat. Trip stops shuffling the cards and places them on the table.

You're a bit long in the tooth to be single.

Val I always make rational decisions, Mr Trip.

A beat.

I like men. I'm not partial to marriage.

Trip The jury, for instance, acted on impulse. They acquitted because their hunch was – and I am speaking off the record you understand – that I was correct. They looked at me and they looked at her and –

Val I'm on your side. Don't misunderstand –

Trip No no no, let me finish – the jury did not need the trial *transcript* to come to their conclusion. They understood the nature of the beast without the need for –

Val Although, I find this line of theorising highly dubious –

Trip – without the need for analysis, without the need for for *articulation.*

Val Well. That blows trials by jury, I guess.

Trip There you go. There you *go.* People like you make a mockery of the system.

Val Which system?

Trip The whole the the – *all* systems, for Chrissake.

A pause.

Val It was a joke. I made a joke.

Trip If you always act rationally, why were you bent over a desk re-enacting a rape?

Val There was no rape, Mr Trip. There was only a beach. Stars. The thrill of it all.

Trip It was a figure of speech.

Val I'm aware of that. I am *aware* – I don't appreciate, Mr Trip – and please understand that I am not being antagonistic here, really I am not – however, I do *not* appreciate what I perceive to be condescension –

Trip (*begins to deal out a hand of Solitaire*) You know, Ms Greco, you are rather attractive when –

Val – I have come here with good intentions. I support your position and I am not I am not willing –

Trip – when you're slightly angry. Yes. Your eyes take on a positively, yes, a positively brilliant aspect, and I must say –

Val – I am not willing to put up with – especially when there are so many, yes, I have to say it, so many inconsistencies in your account – I will not put up with this shit.

A beat.

Anger becoming women is a cliché, Mr Trip.

Trip Nonetheless, it is a much admired cliché, Ms Greco. I felt you might appreciate it as part of the *lore* of popular culture. Which, as you remind me, you so respect. You so so . . . *elevate.*

Val I observe trends. I investigate their validity.

Trip Am I a trend?

Val Well. You're certainly *popular.*

Trip I *am* popular culture.

Val Hold on now, just – surely you can't believe –

Trip No, but I am, Ms Greco. The tide of popular opinion and support rushes my way. It *rushes.* It it –

He studies his Solitaire hand for a moment, realises his mistake.

Red ten on red jack

He corrects his mistake.

Val There are those who say you are a criminal. That your position and your wealth and –

Trip My *position*? What what – what is that? *Position?*

Val Look look. How can I convince you, Mr Trip – my sincerity, my my total belief in your – but my investigative skills would would be lacking –

Trip I am not some some criminal, some poor – I am not jobless and and poor and black like that that *animal* – that what's his name –

Val The the integrity of my scholarship would be sorely doubted if I did not ask – look, I trust you absolutely. There is, believe me, no uncertainty but please tell me why – look look, what are you *doing* with those cards –

Trip *He's* the criminal and what do you *mean* by my position? Am I penalised somehow because –

Val You're making me very nervous. I am very uncomfortable and if you insist on that card game I will I will –

Trip Why? Because I have *money*? Because – well, I don't know – because I am handsome? Healthy? Because *any* woman would be beside herself – in a manner of speaking, you understand – not *every* woman, but perhaps quite a few would be thrilled – oh, for God's sake what's his *name*?

Trip slams what's left of the deck of cards onto the table. Val looks at his Solitaire hand.

Val Myself, I like poker.

A beat.

I don't recall his name. But I know he's doing time.

Trip (*resumes playing his hand*) That's as it should be.

Val His defence was your defence.

Trip That that defenceless woman – the abuse, the gall of that man – black seven on red eight – the unmitigated *gall* –

Val Is there something wrong with your hands, Mr Trip? Is there some kind of – I ask because earlier you, your *handkerchief*, well, I –

Trip I love women – no no don't interrupt – I love women and I cannot support their continued brutalisation at the hands of –

Val You're shorter than you appear to be in photographs.

A beat.

I don't know why that's occurred to me.

Trip (*after a beat*) Do you believe I raped Lucy Parks?

Val No.

Trip Why not?

Val Did you? I mean, if what you're saying is –

Trip (*his attempt at a joke*) Answer mine and I'll answer yours.

Val Listen, I will not engage in semantic games I don't have the –

Trip Lucy Parks and I met by chance. We drank gin and tonics. I taught her to play Solitaire. We flirted in the usual manner. And though I did not find her to be physically – what shall we call it, *compelling* –

Val I've never understood the Solitaire. I've never, I mean, why? Why in the midst of –

Trip – I looked at Lucy Parks and saw on her tired face the years of loneliness spread out like a map of despair, Ms Greco, and I could not refuse, I could not *allow* her –

Val Why why – of course, women are illogical, I appreciate that, even I am susceptible and, Mr Trip, I can't tell you how I despise the weakness of illogical action – but why Lucy Parks would bend over a sand dune to have you check her –

Trip I could not allow her to leave without some – and I remind you that I acted with her consent – I I I was full of of compassion, a deep compassion – she deserved some, and naturally so did I –

Val Her stockings, I just, I really just don't know what to make of – and the Solitaire, I mean you were in a bar, for fuck sake, *drinking* – and *hard* booze, mind you –

Trip There is always a moment of doubt in a sexual encounter, Ms Greco, a a a millisecond when consent might be withdrawn or or or – well, the idea is to get beyond that moment to to surpass that natural doubt and move on to the even more natural state of desire that that lurks everywhere, it it –

Val You understand that I never *never* allow a sexual encounter to progress beyond a stage where I cannot control its outcome, and I find it incomprehensible that Lucy Parks could not could not –

Trip quite suddenly places his fingertips over Val's lips. This should appear to be a gentle, rather than an aggressive, action.

Trip Exactly.

A pause. Trip removes the handkerchief from his breast pocket and once again methodically wipes his hands clean.

Do you play Solitaire, Ms Greco? Oh, I know you prefer a rousing hand of five-card stud, but given your your *background* I find it entirely predictable and so –

Val Don't touch me. Don't you touch me.

A beat.

I am not Lucy Parks, Mr Trip.

Trip Pity.

Trip folds up the handkerchief and replaces it in his breast pocket. A pause.

Val Is there something, is there – why in the *fuck* do you keep wiping your hands, Mr Trip?

Trip When do you expect your book to be published, Ms Greco?

Val Some would say you're being – and I'm not necessarily one of them, I want you to know that – some might say you're being, well, evasive, Mr Trip.

A beat.

I don't know when the book will be – of course it really *should* be published in time for tenure review –

Trip Do you need photographs?

Val You have, what, *pictures* of the the –

Trip Portraits, Ms Greco. Of me.

Val What?

Trip Black and white eight-by-tens. Posed, candids. I'm exceptionally photogenic. My secretary would be happy to –

Val No no, it's really – thank you, Mr Trip. That's very kind of you, but I don't need –

Trip My secretary is quite good about about, you know, *personal* errands. She wrote a lovely note to Lucy Parks when I sent – and I don't mean to be immodest – the cheque.

Val What's this? What are you – you sent her *money*? Is this what you're – no no I feel you must explain –

Trip Lucy Parks lost her job. Her *livelihood*, Ms Greco. I am surprised you're not aware, because you are so on *top* of things that I naturally –

Val I am aware of her difficulty. I am just taken aback by by your –

Trip Generosity?

Val Something like that. Yes.

Trip My secretary wept when she saw the amount of the cheque.

Val Does your secretary have a name?

Trip Yes.

A pause. Trip removes the handkerchief from his pocket and begins to wipe his hands clean.

Sweaty palms.

A beat.

You won't tell anyone, will you?

Blackout.

Scene Two

Val visits with Lucy. The desk and office chairs have been replaced with a kitchen table and two straight-back chairs. There are several neat stacks of mail-order catalogues on the table.

Lucy I've never met a reporter who didn't take notes.

Val I'm not a reporter. I'm a professor.

Lucy You don't look like a teacher.

Val I'm a professor of English literature. Actually.

Lucy Like I said. You don't look like a teacher. Still, you ought to take notes.

Val This is an informal interview, Lucy.

Lucy Do I *know* you?

Val Pardon?

Lucy See. You can't even follow my *questions* without notes. How are you supposed to remember my answers?

A beat.

I'm tired of familiarity. I'd like a little *formality*.

Val You've been through an ordeal, Lucy, and I'd like to make this as –

Lucy Miss Parks.

Val Okay, okay, I only thought – the two of us, we –

Lucy I see. You want girl talk.

Val I had assumed you might be comfortable, *amenable* even to to –

Lucy Amenable?

Val (*searching for synonyms*) Receptive, willing, uhm –

Lucy I know what it means.

Val (*trying to lighten the atmosphere a bit*) So. If I don't look like a teacher, what *do* I look like?

Lucy An asshole.

Val Fine fine. The level of your hostility is perfectly understandable after what you've been through, but the use of obscenity is is –

Lucy I know who you are and why you've come here and and – what do you mean, after what I've *been* through? What do you think I've been *through*?

Val Well. The trial. For one thing. And the the –

Lucy You can't even say it, can you?

A beat.

I'm aware of your *brief*, Professor. And anyway, you read the papers: it never happened.

Val I believe in the efficacy of our legal system, Miss Parks.

Lucy So do I.

Val You do?

Lucy Uh-huh.

Val Good. Good. I'm impressed by your ability to accept –

Lucy I said I believed in its efficacy. I don't accept its infallibility.

Val (*after a beat*) If I could just get a few details, Miss Parks, you know – a little background on your your – you're a grade-school crossing guard with ten years –

Lucy I was.

A beat.

Val. Val Greco. Val *Val* – short for . . .?

Val – with ten years service and and I understand you are single? Never been married? Is that correct?

Lucy Free. For the moment. Too bad, huh, because I'm kind of *past* it, right? Kind of like you, Professor.

A beat.

What *is* Val short for?

Val (*a beat*) Valentina. After my grandmother.

Lucy A real *whopper* of a name. Phew. Hey, listen, I don't blame you for hiding behind a diminutive. So do I. Me, now, *I* was named after a Little Richard song.

Val This is, this is – please, Lucy, I'd really like to talk, to to really *talk* –

Lucy Gal to gal?

A beat.

Miss Parks. I insist.

Val I'm sorry. I've been travelling too much. Aeroplanes make me – look look, aren't you going to offer me a cup of coffee?

Lucy No.

A pause.

Val Tea, then. I'll take tea.

Lucy How much you getting to write this book? More or less than you can stuff into a breadbox?

A pause. Lucy begins flipping through a catalogue.

Val I'm very thirsty.

Lucy I'm a really bad hostess.

Val Look look, Lu – Miss Parks – without your co-operation I will be unable to present a balanced portrait of the complexities of of –

Lucy Complexities? You're talking to me about *complexities*? Listen to *me*, Valentina. Have you any idea – have you any *notion* of what it means to be under public scrutiny – oh oh, well, I guess you *do*, Professor, you've got –

Val My celebrity is a different matter altogether and I resent –

Lucy Oh yes yes yes, you've got, let's see, you've got *rock* stars and and shit-kicking academics from Yale and politicians arguing –

Val I have earned my spotlight in a a decent and time-honoured manner

Lucy Pimply boy-prodigy novelists and wannabe *poetesses* ripping each other's eyes out over your your half-assed ramblings on the virtue of *dicks* –

Val No no, you mustn't – hold on hold on, I have earned public recognition through difficult – and yes, it must be said, ball-breaking scholarship into the –

Lucy So have *I* earned public recognition, Professor. And look where it's got me.

A beat. She flips through a catalogue.

What do you think? A Whirlpool or an Amana fridge-freezer?

Val All right. Let's think this through rationally and with – wait wait. Why *shouldn't* I take advantage of the spotlight cast on me? Why not?

Lucy Because it makes me look ridiculous.

A beat.

The spotlight cast upon me. What a turn of phrase.

Val I'd really like something to drink.

Lucy Nope. All out of drinks. Will you remember to write about my bad table manners in your book? And don't forget to mention my bad haircut which the press – bless their little olive-pit hearts – evidently took as an indication of my latent lesbianism.

Val (*after a beat*) Are you a lesbian? Because, if you are – and I place no judgement on this at all, none whatsoever – I would understand the complications of –

Lucy Wait wait wait wait – you want to know if I'm –

Val The probable emotional difficulties involved in discussing your sexuality after such a traumatic several –

Lucy You want to know if I'm *gay*?

Val (*a beat*) You can tell me.

Lucy You really want to know this? This would be, what? *Helpful* to your research?

Val It has its value. Yes.

Lucy Uh-huh. Well. No. I'm not.

Val You're not. Okay. I don't mind if you don't want –

Lucy I'm not gay. Sorry. Another theory bites –

Val *I* used to be. For a couple of years. Therefore, I really *do* understand the complex nature of –

Lucy No no no, you will not, you will *not* confess. This is not a church, Valentina.

A beat.

Though with your your – how should I put this – with your *views* on us girls I'm not surprised none of us would have you after a couple of years.

Val I didn't say *that.*

Lucy No. You didn't. I did.

Val (*after a beat*) If you would talk about your plans for the future –

Lucy I'm gonna buy a lot of appliances.

Val Fine fine. Appliances. Uhm. What? Kitchen appli –

Lucy Do not patronise me.

A beat.

Your essays on the romantic poets are very entertaining, Valentina.

Val I I – thank you. I'm flattered you read them – and given your hostility towards me I'm surprised you –

Lucy You ought to stick to the romantics. You're a little loopy on the real beasts, though. Like him.

Val I don't know who you're –

Lucy Yes, you do.

A pause. Lucy re-arranges her catalogue piles on the table.

Now. I keep separate piles for electronics, clothing, household goods and and – oh what have we *here* – my newest category: luxury goods.

Val Luxury goods?

Lucy I've gone beyond J. C. Penney and Sears, Professor. Way beyond. Look. Look at this: a combination fax, laptop computer and paper shredder. What do you think?

Val Why did you lose your job? I mean, one reads all sorts –

Lucy Why do *you* think I lost my job?

Val I really couldn't say.

Lucy Then keep reading.

Val (*after a beat*) While I don't necessarily condone the actions taken by your school board, you must understand – and I am being completely objective in my analysis of the of the –

Lucy Objective? What what – is it really, do you you – objectivity isn't *relative*, Professor, it isn't –

Val My analysis of the situation is ob – and look look you cannot fault their concern for the welfare of their students, many of whom are –

Lucy My financial situation wasn't *objective* – how how the *fuck* could you even –

Val Many of whom are young *girls*. Miss Parks: they are very young girls and perhaps the school board's action was a pre-emptive – a a *precaution* against what possibly –

Lucy Oh. Yeah. I forgot about that. Sure sure. Stupid me.

Val I don't mean to suggest I *believe* –

Lucy Well I guess I better be on the horn to *your* school board to tell them about *your* dip in the waters of –

Val They know.

A beat.

And of course, my position isn't controlled by a *school board*. Higher education has its own governing body, Miss Parks, and there is not anything wrong –

Lucy Anyway, it's trendy now. Right?

Val There is some, there is a marked trend – yes – in that direction.

Lucy Can you think of any practical use for a paper shredder? In the home, I mean?

A beat.

The spotlight, Professor, is his. And yours. Me, I'm collecting junk mail and contemplating a better haircut.

Val It's good, really *admirable* that you've kept your sense of humour.

Lucy Must be my working-class upbringing.

Val Have *you* noticed that, too? I mean, the way the working class respond to adversity is is is, well, I can't *begin* to –

Lucy You really know how to shovel the shit.

A pause. Val takes a catalogue and begins to leaf through it.

Val So. What will you do now, Miss Parks?

Lucy Fuck all.

Lucy takes the catalogue away from Val. Her action is not overtly aggressive.

Val Surely that's not healthy, it's not conducive to the process of –

Lucy I've *earned* fuck-all status.

A beat.

You shouldn't touch what's not yours, Valentina.

Val Fair enough.

A beat.

I was not *born* into privilege, Miss Parks. I was not handed my opportunities. I took, I learned, I *strove* for the excellence that was lacking in my environment and my actions entitled me –

Lucy Yeah yeah, I've heard this this – pull-yourself-up from-your-bootstrap stories are passé, Professor. Listen listen, I bet you –

Val No no you don't, you can't compare –

Lucy I bet you all your *entitlement* that I have more cash tucked away for a rainy day – but wait I'm not being fair because well – wink wink – I haven't really *earned* my recent income, have I? I haven't sweated over over literary *trivia* and –

Val Don't you dare compare our our – you foolish –

Lucy I haven't been peering up my own asshole looking for people to to *insult* and and –

Val You lying little – you you *coarse* –

Lucy Lying? *Lying?* I've got half a million bucks stashed away in a dozen bank accounts. How about you?

Val You cashed – wait wait you didn't actually *accept* –

Lucy You go out for what you think is a quiet drink on the beach, you know, just just you and your inconsequential thoughts out there in the night air, with your *bad* haircut –

Val I hadn't – I must admit I hadn't thought, well of course Mr Trip told me he sent he he *mentioned* that he –

Lucy *So.* You go out for a couple of gin and tonics and you wind up with a stack of junk mail and half a million in the bank. Who knew?

A beat.

Mister Trip? *Mister* Trip?

A pause. Val picks up the catalogue she'd leafed through earlier. She leafs through it again, finds what she's looking for and places the open catalogue on the table.

Val I prefer Whirlpool fridge-freezers. Always have.

Lucy (*looks at the catalogue*) That's a nice one. Do you want it?

Val I have – mine is perfectly adequate –

Lucy I can buy you one. I can buy you *ten.*

Val No no no, that's not necessary though it's it's really very *good* of you to –

Lucy What do you think happened to me on that beach? What do you do you –

Val Lucy, I don't – listen, I don't really – I don't believe that anybody can ever *precisely* know –

Lucy Fuck you. All right? Call me *Miss Parks.* Fuck you.

Val (*after a beat*) I was going to say I was was –

Lucy I know. And believe me, I will not bite the hand that's *fed* me, Professor. I know my place. Do you?

Val (*after a beat*) If we could set up another appointment another, a a time when we could –

Lucy I've got plenty of mail-order to slosh through. I'm in no hurry. Why are *you* in such a hurry?

Val Actually I have – I really must catch a flight to to – but I would like to *discuss* with you the the –

Lucy What *what* – the finer points of your just-say-no theory? The the *reasons* why I drank gin that night instead of beer, which – and I've got to say this is my favourite press hunch – which somehow made it clear to him that I was was *ready* for –

Val Look look I'm running late. I'm late. For a television appearance. Really.

Lucy An *appearance*? Is this some kind of a I don't know some kind of a joke or or maybe –

Val No no, I mean I am sincerely running late for a *discussion* –

Lucy Hey hey, I'm so *late* I don't know where time went and what the *fuck* are you talking about on *television*?

Val Well. I'm – it's on the political implications of gender. Actually.

Lucy That old chestnut.

A pause. Lucy picks up the open catalogue.

Listen, *Valentina*. You write down the model number of that Whirlpool and it'll pop up on your doorstep before you know it. Me, I'm gonna make myself a nice hot cup of coffee. You want some?

Val touches Lucy's arm. Several beats before Lucy pulls her arm away. After a beat.

I bet you're the cream and sugar type.

Blackout.

Scene Three

Trip and Lucy at the beach. The kitchen table and straight-back chairs have been replaced with a cocktail table and a couple of nondescript outdoor chairs. A pitcher of gin and tonic and two glasses are on the table. One glass, Trip's, is full, The other hasn't been used. Lucy wears a bright yellow school-crossing guard's raincoat.

Lucy It could rain at any moment.

Trip All right I – did I say anything about it? Did I?

Lucy Okay okay so it's the only – what are you gonna do, *sue* me? I *like* yellow. I can be seen in the dark.

A beat.

You know, there are plenty of tables out here that you could easily – I don't see why you –

Trip Could be Paris. Could be Rome.

Lucy Really, I am sure the waiter would be happy to – what? What about – what are you talking about?

Trip Here. Tonight. Could be Paris. Could be Rome.

Lucy Well, if you're a *jerk* maybe, but –

Trip People sit like this. Together. In Europe.

Lucy We sit like this here, too. Only we tend to *know* the people we sit with.

Trip No no, you don't see what I'm –

Lucy I see it.

A beat.

Lucy This is not my idea of a vacation paradise.

Trip I'm sorry. You're not feeling well. I should have been more sensitive, I know, but the exuberance of –

Lucy I feel fine. My travel agent, however, *isn't* going to feel so hot when I get back home.

Trip You don't – you're not a –

Lucy Local. No. Neither are you.

Trip As a matter of fact, I'm not. How did you –

Lucy Do I look – what's wrong with me? Do I look stupid or something? Do I look *European*?

Trip Maybe I should take this from the – I merely sought to point out that were we in *Paris*, were we two two –

Lucy Ships passing in the night?

Trip Yes. Yes, I see you're a romantic at –

Lucy Yeah, well, I've seen all those ships-passing-in-the-night movies and you know what? They all end badly.

Trip Do they?

Lucy Oh yeah. Real badly.

A beat.

Do they end badly in Europe, too?

A pause. Trip finishes off his drink and pours himself another.

Trip I wasn't – look, I *like* your coat.

Lucy I don't. But it's part of the job.

Trip I wasn't looking at it. I wasn't looking at you – of course, I *was* looking. At you. But but that is only natural as I am *sitting* – and what is your job, Mrs Mrs . . .

Lucy I don't talk shop on vacation.

A beat.

Why do you assume I'm married?

Trip I didn't, I don't – I –

Lucy Yes. You do. You *did.*

Trip I wish you'd share a drink with me. We could be the only two people –

Lucy Oh oh oh, now don't, just don't lay that kind of line –

Trip No no, please, you must – I speak *metaphorically.*

Lucy The insane speak metaphorically. Are you insane?

A pause. Trip pours Lucy a drink

Trip So. I take it you've never been to Europe, Miss, Miss –

Lucy Listen. This, however pathetic it may be, is my *holiday.* My fucking two weeks of fun in the sun. And all right, okay, I can't tell you *why* I've chosen to drag along part of my goddamned uniform except, well, you know it *is* a very fine raincoat –

Trip Your name. Please. I'm just trying to be – listen listen, it's common courtesy and I –

Lucy Oh *please,* mister, I'm so tired and I should have flown here but I can't stand – I can't *afford* – oh fuck I actually *like* Greyhounds and –

Trip suddenly touches his fingertips to Lucy's lips. A beat. He withdraws his hand

Trip I'm Benjamin Trip.

A pause. Lucy downs her drink.

Lucy Touch me again and I'll tear off your face.

A beat.

Jesus. I hate gin and tonic.

Trip I'm Benjamin Trip.

Lucy Do you think maybe a waiter will come by some time this *century* so I can order a beer because, really, I have to tell you, this stuff is –

Trip Did you hear what I said?

Lucy Yes. And I repeat: touch me again and I'll tear off your face.

A beat.

Now, I'd like a beer.

Trip I have just told you that I am –

Lucy Oh and by the way, Mr Trip, I'm Michelle Pfeiffer. Oh sure, I'm looking a bit rough between films, but, hey, on my good days you could –

Trip What do I have to do to convince you that – to make you *understand* that – wait wait – here –

Trip removes his wallet from his inside jacket pocket and holds out his driver's licence for her to see. She tries to take it, as one would naturally. Trip pulls it slightly back.

Please – I really – please don't touch it.

Lucy (*taking a good look at the licence*) Fine. I – no *kidding*. You're that that *guy* with the –

Trip Yes. I am.

Lucy The guy with real estate? The *casinos*?

Trip No no, not him.

Lucy Oh sure, not *him*. You're the one with the –

Trip Yes. Yes. I am he.

Lucy God, the insurance companies – You could knock me *down* – God, I can't *believe* –

Trip No no no no – airlines.

Lucy What?

Trip I'm in *airlines*.

Lucy Oh, right. Airlines, casinos. Yeah.

A beat. Lucy pours herself another drink

So. You're *tha*t guy.

Trip Interesting, no?

Lucy No. It's not interesting.

Trip A happy coincidence, then.

Lucy Well. It certainly is a coincidence.

A beat. She downs her drink

So what's the situation? Some over-eager tour operator sell you a bad trip?

Lucy laughs at her own bad joke. Trip doesn't. A beat.

Trip You're very funny.

Lucy No. I'm very tired. And pissed off at this crummy *resort*.

Trip I like it here.

A beat.

Trip Pour me a drink?

Lucy They have waiters for that.

Trip The waiters are not present

Lucy And I am?

Trip Yes.

Lucy Oh oh, now you can, you can just go and –

Trip I do not mean to – it was – I simply asked you to –

Lucy You want a drink, you want a – is *that* what you want?

Trip Yes. That's all.

Lucy Okay, I'll give you a – *here* – here it *is*.

Lucy pours gin and tonic into Trip's glass. She overpours, and liquid falls into Trip's lap.

Trip What the – that's that's, come on, that's –

Lucy stops pouring.

Lucy I failed home economics.

A pause. Trip ignores the spilled drink in his lap. He calmly sips at his gin and tonic. Lucy laughs.

I'm sorry, I shouldn't be laughing but this is this is – oh *God*, this is just a really bad day. I'm such an *idiot*.

A beat, and Trip joins in the laughter.

Trip You're having a bad day. So? What the hell – we all have bad –

Lucy Yes, we all *do* have – oh my *God*, what did I do to your suit it's it's – the material *alone* would cost what I –

Trip Never mind. Never mind. I deserved it.

Lucy No no, you didn't deserve some *harridan* with a yellow school-crossing guard coat –

Trip Yes, but sometimes I do overstep my – of course, it's a natural extension of – well, a man in my position can sometimes be a tad insensitive to to to –

Lucy My mistake, really – people tell me all the time what a –

Trip Is *that* what you do?

Lucy I – sorry, I don't know –

Trip A school-crossing guard. Is *that* what you are?

Lucy Yes, but how –

Trip The coat. The yellow coat. Of *course.*

Lucy Whoops. Me and my big mouth.

Trip It must be quite an interesting –

Lucy It's not.

A beat. Lucy pours herself another drink

Trip Surely, it's quite a responsible –

Lucy How exactly did you get into the airline business?

Trip From the ground up.

A beat. Lucy laughs.

Lucy Oh man, this is my lucky day, I'll tell you –

Trip What? Did I say something funny?

Lucy (*breaks up again*) Did you – did you – oh, forget it.

A beat.

Do you think you could maybe *fly* a waiter in to bring me a beer?

Trip I'm sorry. I seem to be making a dreadful impression.

Lucy Forget it.

Trip I'd hate to think that *I'm* contributing to your nightmare holiday.

Lucy Listen, it's – oh well, you know – it's not important, it's not – what are *you* doing here, anyway?

Trip I'm having a drink with you.

Lucy Me, now, it makes sense that *me* with my *responsible* little salary and my –

Trip My first business was based here. Electrical cabling. Sprockets.

Lucy *Sprockets?*

Trip Ten-man shop. Three-storey warehouse. Simple. Neat. Sometimes I really miss –

Lucy Oh oh oh, here it comes: sentimentality alert. Please. Spare me the, you know, the –

Trip I don't miss the business. I miss the place. The *location.*

A beat.

I'm never recognised here. There's not a fax machine in sight.

Lucy I'm never recognised here, either.

A pause. Trip pours them both another drink

Trip Isn't it a bit warm for you? In the coat, I mean.

Lucy This? Warm? Nah. It's really kind of –

She pats it down as she speaks.

– substantial, and like I said it could rain at just about –

She finds something in her pocket and removes it. It's a wrapped deck of cards.

Oh. Found these in the toilet.

Trip Pardon?

Lucy Yeah. They were right there in the Greyhound toilet. I thought I – thought, I remembered it was – I don't know – bad luck or something to pass up a wrapped deck of cards.

Trip Bad luck?

Lucy Maybe it's something I picked up in catechism, just one of those –

Trip Do you play?

Lucy I don't know. Do I?

Trip Shall we open them?

Lucy I don't know. Sure.

Trip You're making me warm.

Lucy All right all right –

Trip No no – the coat – it's making me sweat.

Lucy (*after a beat*) Go on. Open the deck.

Trip What shall we play?

Lucy I don't know. Whatever.

Trip Bridge? Well, of course, we need four to –

Lucy *Bridge?* It's a little fancy for –

Trip Okay okay, I know – *baccarat* – no no, that's really –

Lucy Maybe it's not a good – maybe I ought to go –

Trip Old Maid.

A beat.

Trip Do you know that one?

A pause.

Lucy Now that you mention it, I'm really – maybe I *am* a little warm with the coat but I had this accident –

Trip You had a – you're *hurt*?

Lucy No no, I had this – I was in the toilet, on the bus, and you know how sometimes you see things, well, you really don't see them fully but perhaps out of the corner of your eye –

Trip Quite. Quite. I sometimes –

Lucy And I saw this, I don't – who *knows* what I thought it was but I thought it was moving like some – it could have been an animal, a rodent, or or –

Trip I *hate* when that happens.

Lucy Or who knows, but – well I didn't *want* to know so I whipped around and caught my leg, I caught my *stocking* on the edge –

Trip Oh how horrible –

Lucy The edge of the metal, what do you call – the *waste* bin and well, it's torn all the way up to –

Trip I understand. Yes.

Lucy And it's a funny thing but I really feel somehow exposed or –

Trip Naked.

Lucy Yes, with the – without stockings.

A beat.

Lucy I'm kind of old-fashioned. So. So that's why – that's why I'm wearing –

Trip The coat.

Lucy Precisely.

A beat.

I've always wanted to learn how to play Solitaire. Sounds like a good one to know for a, you know –

Trip A rainy day?

Lucy Yeah. That's right.

Trip Can I see?

Lucy Can you –

Trip The stocking. I might be able to repair –

Lucy I doubt it.

Trip (*after a beat*) I know all the Solitaire variations.

Lucy You're a versatile guy. Sprockets. Card games. Stockings.

A beat.

I wish I had a camera. Right now.

Trip Why?

Lucy Don't know really.

Trip (*reaching for the pitcher of G and Ts*) Perhaps you'd like – you'd maybe consider – oh, I don't know *what* I'm –

Trip knocks over the pitcher. A beat. He begins to sob.

Lucy Hey hey now, what the – come on, now – we could get some –

Trip I've made such a such a goddamned *fool* of myself out here.

Lucy No no no, don't even think – listen, I'm really a terrible bitch but it's –

Trip It's just – I'm so *isolated*, you see, and striking up a conversation with a perfectly *ordinary* – oh God, you think I'm some kind of a –

Lucy But it's only my self-preservation *instinct* kicking in – don't take any notice –

Trip I should go I should pay the – oh, why do I *bother* –

Trip begins to shiver.

Lucy Hey hey, wait a min – where the *hell* are the waiters when you need them – are you okay are you gonna be – oh, here here –

Lucy removes her coat and puts it over Trip's shoulders.

Is that better? Is that – oh, come on – yes yes, breathe deeply breathe – yeah, that's right that's – you're fine fine.

A pause. Trip stops crying.

Trip You have lovely legs.

Lucy (*after a beat*) I've never seen a man like – listen, you're just too *rich* or something to cry. Okay?

A beat.

I don't have lovely legs. But thanks anyway.

Trip I meant no –

Lucy None taken. I better – will you be all right to get – I don't know – wherever you're going?

Trip My car is over –

Lucy Is that yours? The big black what? BMW?

Trip Mercedes convertible.

Lucy Over there – on the beach, that one?

Trip Yes. I like driving on sand. Makes me feel young.

Lucy You're not so old.

Trip I'm old enough.

Lucy Aren't we all.

Trip I'm sorry to be such a bother. I usually am much more able –

Lucy No no no, it's too late in the evening for apologies and – are you okay – you still got the shakes?

Trip It's been a long day.

Lucy Yeah. It's been long.

Lucy walks towards the endless horizon. Trip watches her. A pause as she looks out towards the beach.

I'll never understand why I talked myself into a beach vacation. I *hate* sand.

She turns towards Trip. He sits comfortably, Lucy's coat wrapped around him. He watches her.

What are you waiting for? Come on. On your feet.

Trip (*regarding the coat*) The shoulders are perfect.

Lucy Up and at 'em. Well. Come on. Come closer.

Lucy gestures to Trip. A beat, then:

Blackout.

End of play.